great dates

Unique, Fun & Meaningful Dating Ideas

Michael & Tiffany Ross

BARBOUR
PUBLISHING

For

Philip Larson

Cover and interior design and illustration by Julie Doll.

Published by Barbour Publishing, Inc., P.O. Box 719, Uhrichsville, Ohio 44683, www.barbourbooks.com

Our mission is to publish and distribute inspirational products offering exceptional value and biblical encouragement to the masses.

 Member of the
Evangelical Christian
Publishers Association

Printed in China.
5 4 3 2 1

CONTENTS

How to Use This Book

It's an all-too familiar scene: You meet that special someone and your heart takes a trip to cloud nine. But then comes the reality of the actual date! Your brain suddenly floods with all kinds of catastrophic possibilities: What if my tongue gets tied up in knots every time I speak? What if I do something stupid? And speaking of doing stuff, I have no idea about how we should spend our time! What if this date ends up being a huge disaster?

Dating shouldn't trigger more fear than a dentist appointment. If you're ready to get off the emotional roller coaster, this little book might be the most important one you'll read all year.

Whether you're practically an expert or feeling clueless with the opposite sex, these pages contain tons of helpful stuff: step-by-step plans, tips for making a lasting impression, and dozens of creative ideas—dates under twenty dollars, adventure dates, cultured dates, and more.

So, don't hold back! Put the fun back into dating, connect through meaningful conversation, and explore creative activities together.

Inside, you'll find:

WHAT YOU'LL NEED—supplies required for each dating idea

$$$-AN ESTIMATED COST OF EACH DATE—
$ Cheap (under $10),
$$ Inexpensive ($10 to $20),
$$$ Moderate ($20 to $75),
$$$$ Expensive (over $75)

GO ONLINE—where to look on the Internet for more ideas

GREAT DATE DETAILS—step-by-step instructions for planning and pulling off an ideal date

Finally, brothers, whatever is true,
whatever is noble, whatever is right,
whatever is pure, whatever is lovely,
whatever is admirable—
if anything is excellent or praiseworthy—
think about such things.

PHILIPPIANS 4:8

CHAPTER 1
Dates under Twenty Dollars

Short on cash? Don't sweat it!
The truth is, you don't have
to take out a loan to impress
your date. Creativity and
thoughtfulness are the keys to
a truly great time. This chapter
is packed with of low-cost
ideas that can result in high
returns: lots of smiles, good
memories, a relationship that's
focused on connecting with each
other—not shelling out cash.

Have Fun in a Pumpkin Patch

The opportunity to visit a pumpkin farm only comes along a few short weeks in a year. Plan ahead and enjoy the crisp autumn air.

WHAT YOU'LL NEED

- *directions to and the hours of operation of a local pumpkin farm*
- *possibly an appointment*
- *comfortable shoes*
- *light jackets*
- *camera (optional)*

\$\$ INEXPENSIVE (\$10 TO \$20)

GO ONLINE

Key Internet search words: Pumpkin Farms, Autumn Decorations, Local Harvest

GREAT DATE DETAILS

Step 1: *Find out the hours, fees, and directions to a local pumpkin farm.*

Step 2: *Ask your date to wear comfortable clothes, shoes he or she doesn't mind getting dirty, and a jacket.*

Step 3: *Pick up your date and head to the pumpkin patch.*

Step 4: *Enjoy the outdoors as you walk around looking for just the right pumpkin. Find a few extra for carving or for decorating the front yard, your desk at work, or your kitchen table.*

Step 5: *Take your time enjoying the fresh air. Snap a few photos of the beautiful autumn colors.*

Step 6: *Cap off the day with a warm cup of cider.*

Enjoy
a Kid's Meal
(Big~Kid Style)

Whether or not you grew up eating in fast-food restaurants, this experience will take you back to your childhood. The meals are relatively small, but the toys have come a long way.

WHAT YOU'LL NEED

- *ability to drive or walk to any local fast-food restaurant*
- *fun attitude around a lot of kids*
- *everyday clothing*
- *small to average appetite*
- *camera (optional)*

$ CHEAP (UNDER $10)

GO ONLINE

Key Internet search words: McDonalds, Wendy's, Burger King, Subway, Sonic Drive-In

GREAT DATE DETAILS

Step 1: *Prep your date that he or she is about to step back into his or her childhood.*

Step 2: *Pick the fast-food restaurant of choice and head out.*

Step 3: *Upon arrival, order a kid's meal for each of you.*

Step 4: *Sit in the play area (if available) and enjoy your pint-sized meal.*

Step 5: *Take time to watch the children playing and reminisce about your favorite childhood memories.*

Step 6: *At the end of your meal, give your toys away to a couple of the little ones running around.*

Make a Date with Night Court

This puts a new spin on checking out the nightlife. Night court is a great way to see your police and judicial systems at work. Please note that the interesting cases usually don't roll in until around midnight.

WHAT YOU'LL NEED

- *a town that holds night court*
- *information on the location and the best place to park*
- *comfortable clothing*
- *no food, beverage, or cameras allowed*
- *basic interest in law enforcement*
- *coins for the parking meter*

$ CHEAP (UNDER $10)

GO ONLINE

Key Internet search words: Night Court, Local Justice Department, 24-Hour Court Proceedings, Sheriff's Department

GREAT DATE DETAILS

Step 1: *Check out the location and availability of parking beforehand. Your local police station can usually offer sound advice.*

Step 2: *After grabbing a late-night snack, head downtown for night court. There's usually not much activity until around midnight.*

Step 3: *Plug the meter, head indoors, and find a comfortable seat.*

Step 4: *This is kind of a hit or miss shot. Sometimes the court is full and very entertaining. Other times, it's slow and uneventful.*

Step 5: *Remember, no food, drinks, or cameras are allowed.*

Step 6: *Allow time for a cup of coffee afterward to recap the experience.*

Visit a Nursing Home

If you have never been to a nursing home, now is a good time to start. Not only will you bring a smile to someone else's face, but you will inevitably hear a few funny stories along the way.

WHAT YOU'LL NEED

- *previous arrangements worked out with a local nursing home*
- *directions*
- *any small gifts to hand out*
- *casual dress*

$ CHEAP (UNDER $10)

GO ONLINE

Key Internet search words: Volunteer Opportunities, Local Retirement Homes

GREAT DATE DETAILS

Step 1: *Most retirement communities and nursing homes have an ongoing list of activities for their residents. Call ahead and volunteer to be Saturday morning helping hands. This is also the time to explain that you and your date wish to participate together.*

Step 2: *Don't worry, you won't be left alone in a situation you can't handle. Most activities take place in a recreation room or cafeteria full of nurses and staff who are trained caregivers.*

Volunteers can help: call numbers at bingo night, play checkers, push the residents in wheelchairs to and from the rec room, look at photos of grandchildren, hand out gifts, cut and serve a birthday cake, play Ping-Pong, listen to stories.

Step 3: *Take along a few small gifts to hand out to your new friends.*

Step 4: *As your time draws to a close, be sure to thank the residents and staff members for allowing you to spend some time with them. Most likely, they will want you to return soon.*

Ride a Bus— Anywhere

This date offers a chance to be spontaneous while exploring the world of mass transit. Grab a map and let someone else do the driving.

WHAT YOU'LL NEED

- *local bus schedule*
- *city map*
- *correct change*
- *comfortable clothes*

$$ INEXPENSIVE ($10 TO $20)

GO ONLINE

Key Internet search words: Mass Transit, Bus Schedules, Bus Rates and Fares

GREAT DATE DETAILS

Step 1: *Pick up a bus schedule for your town. Read all of the information pertaining to fares, transfers, and area of coverage.*

Step 2: *After picking up your date, walk to the nearest bus stop. If you have to drive, pick the closest stop you can find.*

Step 3: *Review the map and schedule, and pick where you want to go.*

Step 4: *You could go to a park for a walk, downtown for fun photo opportunities, or a specific restaurant for lunch.*

Step 5: *Be sure to ask if you will need a transfer token for a connecting bus.*

Step 6: *Sit back and enjoy the ride. Maybe you'll find a new part of town and spontaneously change your plans for the day. Just be sure you know when the last bus leaves your stop. Remember, you are totally dependent upon the mass transit system to get you home.*

Hold a Build-a-Snowman Contest

Get creative with a few household items as you bring life to a snowman (or "snowwoman"). This is truly one of the safest ways to enjoy a good snowstorm.

WHAT YOU'LL NEED

- *warm clothes including hat and gloves*
- *lots of snow*
- *any items around the house for the snowman's eyes, hat, nose, mouth, buttons*
- *camera*
- *hot cocoa (optional)*

$ CHEAP (UNDER $10)

GO ONLINE

Key Internet search words: Winter Games, Snowmen, Hot Cocoa

GREAT DATE DETAILS

Step 1: *You can only have this contest when there is plenty of snow.*

Step 2: *After both you and your date are warmly dressed, set a time limit for the contest. Forty-five minutes is reasonable.*

Step 3: *Split up, hit the outdoors, and start building your snowmen.*

Step 4: *Use any household item you can find for the eyes, nose, hat, buttons, and arms.*

Step 5: *When the time is up, step back and view each other's snowmen. Pull out the camera before they begin to melt or before the borrowed items for the face need to go back into the house.*

Step 6: *It doesn't really matter who wins, but you can let your friends or family make that decision while the two of you warm up inside with a cup of hot cocoa.*

Enjoy Some Major Fun at a Minor League Game

Baseball can be exciting at any level. But it's great to watch minor league players battle it out for a spot in the majors. And the roasted peanuts are a must.

WHAT YOU'LL NEED

- *schedule of local games*
- *directions to the ball field*
- *comfortable clothes*
- *light jackets/sunscreen*
- *camera (optional)*

$$ INEXPENSIVE ($10 TO $20)

GO ONLINE

Key Internet search words: Minor League Baseball, Tickets, Today's Weather

GREAT DATE DETAILS

Step 1: *Check the game schedule for your local team to determine which game to attend.*

Step 2: *Check the weather forecast. This information will help you know how to dress and whether you will need an umbrella or sunscreen.*

Step 3: *Pick up your date and head to the ball field.*

Step 4: *If you have already bought your tickets, check at the box window to see if you can upgrade them.*

Step 5: *Once you have found your seats, make sure you load up on hot dogs, peanuts, cotton candy, and soda.*

Step 6: *Sit back and enjoy the game.*

Play Putt~Putt

It's amazing how much fun it is to putt brightly colored golf balls around on artificial grass. Test your skill as you navigate windmills, streams, elephants, and any other obstacle that stands in your way.

WHAT YOU'LL NEED

- *directions to your local putt-putt course*
- *casual attire*
- *camera (optional)*

$$ INEXPENSIVE ($10 TO $20)

GO ONLINE

Key Internet search words: Putt-Putt, Miniature Golf, Today's Weather

GREAT DATE DETAILS

Step 1: *Research your local miniature golf courses to find the right one for your date.*

Step 2: *Let your date know that you will be outside and he or she should dress accordingly.*

Step 3: *Since most putt-putt courses have more than one course, try to fit in two or three games.*

Step 4: *If you just don't want the fun to stop, step inside and try out a few video games or a round of air hockey.*

Step 5: *Wrap up the date with a splurge at the snack bar.*

Go on a Hayride

Ahh, the smell of hay, fallen leaves, and the crisp outdoors as you ride around in an open-bed truck. There's nothing like an old fashioned hayride.

WHAT YOU'LL NEED

- *usually, this activity is only available during the autumn*
- *warm clothes*
- *camera (recommended)*
- *Note: Make sure your date isn't allergic to hay, horses, or autumn foliage before you head out on this trip.*

$$ INEXPENSIVE ($10 TO $20)

GO ONLINE

Key Internet search words: Autumn Activities, Hayrides, Today's Weather, Local Livery, Local Retreat Centers

GREAT DATE DETAILS

Step 1: *Ask your friends or family for recommendations to the best hayrides in the area.*

Step 2: *It is best to visit beforehand with those conducting the hayride to check out the truck, route, and all-around conditions. At this time, ask about any other services they may offer, like a bonfire, hot cocoa, or horseback rides.*

Step 3: *Dress for chilly autumn nights, and don't forget the camera.*

Step 4: *Get there early to get the best seats (usually up by the cab).*

Step 5: *If the hayride company doesn't offer hot refreshments afterward, head to a coffee shop.*

Play Laser Tag

Strap on some laser tag gear and go commando. You'll find your competitive side as you run, hide, crawl and shoot at anything that moves.

WHAT YOU'LL NEED

- *appetite for something different*
- *blue jeans, T-shirt, and tennis shoes*
- *physical ability to move, crawl, and run around wearing laser tag equipment*

$$ INEXPENSIVE ($10 TO $20)

GO ONLINE

Key Internet search words: Laser Tag, Indoor Tag, War Games

GREAT DATE DETAILS

Step 1: *Realize that this sport isn't only for teens. Folks of all ages and ability levels are welcome.*

Step 2: *Let your date know what he or she is in for.*

Step 3: *Once you're in agreement, put on some comfortable clothes and head out to the laser tag arena.*

Step 4: *Ask the employees for any and all advice they have to offer.*

Step 5: *Take time to familiarize yourself with your equipment.*

Step 6: *Don't hold back. Go for it like your life depends on it.*

Go Bowling

Cash in on those bowling classes they made you take in junior high. Alleys are easy to find and relatively inexpensive. Today, most are even smoke free.

WHAT YOU'LL NEED

- *comfortable clothes*
- *bowling shoes (can be rented at the alley)*
- *camera (optional)*

$$ INEXPENSIVE ($10 TO $20)

GO ONLINE

Key Internet search words: Bowling, Indoor Games, Basics of Bowling

GREAT DATE DETAILS

Step 1: *The biggest preparation for bowling is deciding to go. All ages and skill levels are welcomed.*

Step 2: *Dress comfortably and avoid wearing holey socks. Bowling shoes are required and can be rented at the alley.*

Step 3: *Pick a ball that fits your hand and isn't too heavy. Trim nails before playing to avoid a nasty break.*

Step 4: *You can review how to keep score beforehand, but most alleys automatically keep score for you.*

Step 5: *The only way to improve your bowling score is through practice. So plan on two or three games.*

Step 6: *For the full experience, don't forget the cheeseburgers and fries.*

Play Frisbee Golf

Frisbee and golf. Two outdoor pastimes that have been combined into one great outdoor game. It can be as competitive or relaxing as you want to make it.

WHAT YOU'LL NEED

- *directions and fees to a local Frisbee golf course*
- *Frisbees designed specifically for golf*
- *outdoor clothes*
- *pen and paper for scorekeeping*

$$ INEXPENSIVE ($10 TO $20)

GO ONLINE

Key Internet search words: Frisbee Golf, Parks and Recreation, Local Weather

GREAT DATE DETAILS

Step 1: *Go online or call your parks system to find the location and cost for local Frisbee golf courses.*

Step 2: *Most courses are free and open to the public, but if there is a fee, you will probably have to make a reservation or prepay before game time.*

Step 3: *Gather your Frisbee golf discs from any sports store if you need to purchase them.*

Step 4: *After checking the weather, put on comfortable clothes and shoes, and head outside.*

Step 5: *Keep paper and pen with you to keep score.*

Step 6: *Don't get too competitive. The goal is to spend time together outdoors.*

Feed the Animals at a Kennel

Calling all animal lovers! Kennels are full of our furry, feathered, and even scaly friends. Share some time together helping these animals feel loved.

WHAT YOU'LL NEED

- *prior arrangements with the kennel*
- *comfortable clothes*
- *fresh change of clothes*
- *love for animals*

$ CHEAP (UNDER $10)

GO ONLINE

Key Internet search words: Humane Society, Veterinarian Services, Animal Kennels and Shelters, Volunteer Agencies

GREAT DATE DETAILS

Step 1: *Contact a few kennels to see who might need extra help.*

Step 2: *Ask your date if he or she is allergic to or afraid of animals.*

Step 3: *Talk to the kennel managers and agree on a time frame and the services you'll be providing.*

Step 4: *Make a concentrated effort to perform all the tasks alongside your date. Remember, you're there to spend time together, not bond with a lost puppy.*

Step 5: *Change into fresh clothes if necessary and get a bite to eat afterward.*

Volunteer at a School

It's always insightful to watch your date interact with a child. Discover how they would act with thirty or forty of them. Volunteer during reading time or as field trip chaperones at a local grade school.

WHAT YOU'LL NEED

- *prior approval from school administrators*
- *appropriate clothing*
- *an understanding that you are volunteering as a couple and wish to perform tasks together*
- *money for snacks, drinks, or even lunches*

$ CHEAP (UNDER $10)

GO ONLINE

Key Internet search words: Local Elementary Schools, Volunteer Opportunities, Literacy Programs

GREAT DATE DETAILS

Step 1: *Contact an elementary school and ask if they have any volunteer programs. If they do, ask about the application process.*

Step 2: *After you are both registered and approved to work with the children, request a copy of the upcoming events schedule. It could include book readers, field trip chaperones, playground helpers, ushers for a play or concert, or classroom decorators.*

Step 3: *Once you have agreed on an event, call the school and volunteer.*

Step 4: *Arrive at the event as a couple, and try to pick tasks that will allow you to work side by side with your date.*

Step 5: *Jump in and have fun.*

Attend a Christmas Musical

The sounds of Christmas, both old and new, are full of joyous and celebratory themes. Church choirs everywhere invest a lot of time and energy preparing for cantatas full of songs and drama. Take a break from Christmas shopping and enjoy the music.

WHAT YOU'LL NEED

- *information on local Christmas cantatas*
- *festive clothing*

$ CHEAP (UNDER $10, BUT MANY ARE FREE)

GO ONLINE

Key Internet search words: Community Events, Christmas Cantatas, Holiday Festivities, Christian Churches

GREAT DATE DETAILS

Step 1: *Check out the listing of local Christmas events. Specifically look for cantatas.*

Step 2: *Contact the church to see if there is a charge or if free tickets are available.*

Step 3: *Contact your date and lock in the time. Agree to wear festive clothing like red, green, or white.*

Step 4: *Arrive early so you can get good seats, and then sit back and relax.*

Step 5: *Plan to go out for dessert afterward. You might even want to invite new friends along whom you met at the cantata.*

Pick Blueberries

Most regions in the United States produce blueberries. Farms, vineyards, and orchards open their doors to the public during the late summer. For a small fee, you can pick and enjoy berries fresh off the bush.

WHAT YOU'LL NEED

- *directions to a local blueberry farm, vineyard, or orchard*
- *casual attire and comfortable shoes or boots*
- *gloves to keep your fingers clean (optional)*

$$ INEXPENSIVE ($10 TO $20)

GO ONLINE

Key Internet search words: Blue-berries, Local Farms, Open to the Public Berry Picking

GREAT DATE DETAILS

Step 1: *Find an establishment that grows blueberries. Fresh blueberries are worth a day trip.*

Step 2: *Find out the hours they're open to the public.*

Step 3: *Grab your buckets and head out to the farm.*

Step 4: *Pick more than you need since they make great gifts. Just keep in mind that you usually pay by the pound.*

Step 5: *Also remember that freezing blueberries before you wash them helps them to maintain their shape upon thawing.*

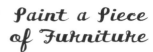

Paint a Piece of Furniture

Repairing a piece of furniture is very rewarding. Even if you simply apply a layer of paint, you will both feel a sense of accomplishment. You will be reminded of your team effort every time you pass that end table, chair, or bench.

WHAT YOU'LL NEED

- *piece of furniture to paint*
- *painting clothes*
- *drop cloth*
- *paint(s)*
- *paint brushes*
- *paint cleaner (for your hands)*
- *camera for before and after shots*

$$ INEXPENSIVE ($10 TO $20)

GO ONLINE

Key Internet search words: Creative Paint Colors, Furniture Renewal Tips, Garage Sales, Flea Markets

GREAT DATE DETAILS

Step 1: *Pick a piece of furniture that needs a new look. If you don't have one, buy one from a yard sale or flea market.*

Step 2: *Scour your garage, closet, or storage unit for paint, brushes, drop cloths, and other needed supplies. Purchase any necessary items you don't have on hand.*

Step 3: *Pick an outside location on a sunny, warm day. The temperature must be above fifty degrees for paint to dry properly.*

Step 4: *Paint away! Try different colors and styles.*

Step 5: *Kick back, enjoy an iced tea, and admire your work.*

Go Beachcombing

Location, location, location. If you're lucky enough to live near a beach, take advantage of your good fortune. It's hard to match the relaxing sound of waves breaking on the sand.

WHAT YOU'LL NEED

- *good weather*
- *extra change of clothes*
- *bucket to carry seashells in*
- *sunscreen, snacks, blanket, and water*
- *camera (recommended)*

$ CHEAP (UNDER $10)

GO ONLINE

Key Internet search words: Parks and Recreation, Local Weather, Oceanfront Activities Schedule

GREAT DATE DETAILS

Step 1: *If the weather is good, head out to the beach.*

Step 2: *Any strip of beach will do, but try to find a less populated area if possible.*

Step 3: *Take your time looking for seashells. Allow the conversation to bounce around between memories, wishes, dreams, and anything else that comes up.*

Step 4: *Pull out the snacks and take a break. There's no hurry—the ocean isn't going anywhere.*

Step 5: *Once you get back home, wash the seashells and divide them among the two of you. A fun souvenir from a great day at the beach.*

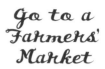

Go to a Farmers' Market

Get on the organic kick and support local farmers by shopping at the farmers' market. You just might find out how a real tomato tastes.

WHAT YOU'LL NEED

- *list of local farmers' markets and hours*
- *comfortable shoes*
- *hunger for fresh fruits and vegetables*

$ CHEAP (UNDER $10)

GO ONLINE

Key Internet search words: Local Farms, Farmer's Markets, Organic Outlets, Fruits and Vegetables Purchasing Tips

GREAT DATE DETAILS

Step 1: *Pick which farmers' market fits your schedules.*

Step 2: *Make a list of fruits or vegetables you're interested in purchasing.*

Step 3: *Stroll the booths tasting samples and comparing prices before you decide what to buy.*

Step 4: *Take your purchases home, wash them well, and enjoy.*

Buy Music Together

When was the last time you purchased a CD? Add a twist by purchasing a CD together that neither of you has heard.

WHAT YOU'LL NEED

- *music store*
- *CD player*
- *an hour of listening time*

$$ INEXPENSIVE (\$10 TO \$20)

GO ONLINE

Key Internet search words: Music Stores, Music Outlets, Music Reviews

GREAT DATE DETAILS

Step 1: *Hop in the car together and head to the music store.*

Step 2: *Pick out one CD neither has ever heard.*

Step 3: *Listen to the music while reading the lyrics.*

Step 4: *Hold your comments until the end. Then, share about the music, the message, and overall impression.*

Step 5: *If your date loves the disc, you could offer it as a gift.*

You alone are the Lord.
You made the heavens,
even the highest heavens,
and all their starry host,
the earth and all that is on it,
the seas and all that is in them.
You give life to everything,
and the multitudes of heaven worship you.

Nehemiah 9:6

CHAPTER 2
Adventure Dates

If your date and you crave
adrenaline-charging adventure,
this is a must-read chapter.
Some of these ideas will
pump up your relationship.
Some will pump up your heart rate.
But we guarantee all of them will
spark an atmosphere of fun.

Hit the Trail

From Acadia to Yosemite, the United States is filled with breath-taking places to hike. Trails weave through canyons and mountains and below waterfalls. Each step inspires romance.

WHAT YOU'LL NEED

- *map, compass, and whistle*
- *hiking boots and proper clothes (dress in layers)*
- *pack filled with essentials: water bottle, energy-boosting snacks, sunscreen, sunglasses*
- *money for park admission*
- *camera*

$$ INEXPENSIVE ($10 TO $20)

GO ONLINE

Key Internet search words: Day Hikes, National Parks

GREAT DATE DETAILS

Step 1: *Locate a trail near home.*

Step 2: *Check weather conditions.*

Step 3: *Fill a pack with hiking essentials.*

Step 4: *Let someone know where you're going and when you expect to return.*

Step 5: *Grab your gear and hit the trail.*

Go Spelunking

Deep. Dark. Dirty. The eerie world of caves is both fascinating and educational—not to mention a place packed with mystery and adventure. But beware: Spelunking is an activity that will take you out of your comfort zone as you hike (and sometimes crawl) by the light of a headlamp. Above all, this date is recommended only for "nonclaustrophobic" folks.

WHAT YOU'LL NEED

- *warm clothing—usually noncotton items, which dry more easily*
- *hiking boots—preferably waterproof*
- *spelunking gear, rentable from a professional guide*
- *snacks*
- *signed parent or guardian release form if you are under eighteen years of age*

\$\$\$ MODERATE (\$20 TO \$75)

 GO ONLINE

Key Internet search words:
Adventure Tours, Caving, Local
Attractions, Spelunking

 GREAT DATE DETAILS

Step 1: *Spelunking can be physi-*
cally demanding, so make sure
you and your date are up for the
challenge.

Step 2: *Once you have found a qualified guide,*
ask him or her for a detailed packing list for
the day.

Step 3: *Ask your guide for a private tour.*
Remember: This is a time to get to know your
date, not a group of tourists.

Step 4: *Review safety tips at your library or on*
the Web.

Step 5: *Dress warm, eat a big breakfast, and*
prepare to get a bit muddy.

Note: Enter a cave only with a professional guide.

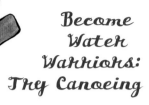

Become Water Warriors: Try Canoeing

Whether on a placid pond or a turbulent river, canoeing isn't all that difficult. It offers scenery, a moderate workout, and time to talk.

WHAT YOU'LL NEED

- *canoe with two oars*
- *life vests*
- *proper attire: swimming suits, sunglasses, sunblock*
- *safety lesson from a professional*

$$$ MODERATE ($20 TO $75)

GO ONLINE

Key Internet search words: Canoe Rentals, River Recreation, Water Sports

GREAT DATE DETAILS

Step 1: *Find a store or recreation center that rents canoes. Consider a safety lesson.*

Step 2: *We recommend an afternoon on a lake or a reservoir. If you're athletic (and experienced in a canoe), take on a river. Make arrangements for someone to pick you up downriver.*

Explore the World Down Under: Go Snorkeling

Warm regions such as Hawaii, Florida, Southern California, the Caribbean, and Mexico offer some of the best snorkeling experiences. But just about any clear lake or river—even a pool—can become a fun snorkeling adventure for you and your date.

WHAT YOU'LL NEED

- *snorkels and flippers*
- *safe, clear body of water*
- *sunscreen*
- *swimsuits*

$$$ MODERATE ($20 TO $75)

GO ONLINE

Key Internet search words: Snorkeling, Water Sports

GREAT DATE DETAILS

Step 1: *Rent, buy, or borrow two sets of snorkels and flippers. (Consider getting a safety demonstration, depending upon where you plan to swim.)*

Step 2: *Slather on sunscreen, take a deep breath, and have fun!*

Take a Midnight Hike

A moonlit, pine-scented trail under an explosion of stars—midnight hikes top the romance scale! While we don't want to spoil the moment, we highly recommend experiencing this kind of adventure date with a group—especially with a professional guide.

WHAT YOU'LL NEED

- *wilderness location unspoiled by "light pollution"*
- *professional guide*
- *flashlights*
- *appropriate shoes and clothing*

$$ INEXPENSIVE ($10 TO $20)

GO ONLINE

Key Internet search words: National Park Events, Wilderness Hikes

GREAT DATE DETAILS

Step 1: *If you live near a national park, you stand a better chance of pulling off this date. Call the National Park Service (or go online) and inquire about midnight hikes.*

Step 2: *Gather some friends or family to accompany you, then make a date to hit the trail.*

Step 3: *Drive to your selected wilderness location and hit the trail.*

Blast the Breakers: Go White~Water Rafting

Your nerves surge with ten thousand volts of raw fear. Your heart pounds, your eyes bulge, your vocal cords explode with a primordial scream loud enough to trigger a Himalayan avalanche. This is what a high-action, bone-jarring white-water encounter feels like. The truth is, river running offers a prime summertime rush—not to mention an ideal adventure date!

WHAT YOU'LL NEED

- *at least a Class III or Class IV river*

- *professional white-water rafting company*

- *polypropylene or Capilene shirts and swimsuits (many outfitters supply these)*
- *extra change of clothes*

$$$ MODERATE ($20 TO $75)

GO ONLINE

Key Internet search words: River Running, White-Water Rafting

GREAT DATE DETAILS

Step 1: *Contact a professional rafting service and schedule a trip. Usually late spring and early summer are the best times to go.*

Step 2: *Be willing to get scared, soaked, and seriously psyched to go again!*

Splat!
Play a Game of Paintball

Air-gun competition, Survival Game, Total Elimination, Capture the Flag—paintball. Regardless of what it's called, and despite its use of semiautomatic paint shooters, most paintball enthusiasts insist that this game is all about fun, not violence. Hey, can 10 million players be wrong? Join the craze and learn how your date reacts under pressure.

WHAT YOU'LL NEED

- *paintball shooters*
- *goggles*
- *pack of gel caps*
- *padding (if you're a wimp, that is)*
- *location to play*

$$$ MODERATE ($20 TO $75)

GO ONLINE

*Key Internet search words:
Capture the Flag, Paintball*

GREAT DATE DETAILS

Step 1: *Locate a paintball gaming center in your town. Note: Indoor facilities are popping up in refurbished warehouses.*

Step 2: *Learn a few facts about the sport. For example, more than twenty-one different paintball games exist. The most popular by far is Capture the Flag.*

Step 3: *Be prepared for slight pain. Players peg each other with gel caps of water-based paint that travel 250 feet per second from the barrel of a paintball shooter. Pellets are fired from various models of air guns, all of which are powered by carbon dioxide (CO_2) charges. And when someone is hit, not only does it sting, but the player is eliminated from the game.*

Climb a Wall—Blindfolded

You slide your hand across a boulder and feel a tiny crevice. You grip it with your fingertips and push with your legs. Inching up a climbing wall, you begin to trust the safety harness around your waist. You discover that the risk isn't too crazy. The scary part is wearing a blindfold. That's right, in this unique twist on climbing, a bandanna covers your eyes! Your date (and climbing partner) acts as your eyes, coaching you from below. He or she calls up instructions and points out handholds. This experience challenges you to (1) listen, (2) communicate, and (3) trust. Note: This activity requires the supervision of a professional climber.

WHAT YOU'LL NEED

- *safe climbing wall*
- *appropriate equipment (usually provided at climbing facilities) safety harness, crampons, climbing shoes*
- *bandanna*
- *professional supervision*

$$ INEXPENSIVE ($10 TO $20)

GO ONLINE

Key Internet search words: Climbing Gyms, Rock Climbing

GREAT DATE DETAILS

Step 1: *Locate a climbing facility that will allow you to climb blindfolded.*

Step 2: *After your climb, discuss what you learned: Was it tough to trust your partner while dangling one hundred feet from the ground—blindfolded? What does this experience teach you about your relationship with Christ? (What does it mean to be belayed—or supported—by the Holy Spirit? How does God point out solid holds in life? How does He catch us when we fall?)*

Learn to Snowboard

If you can resist feeling self-conscious around your date—and count your first day on the slopes as the toughest—the two of you will have a good time mastering this sport together. Snowboarding has a really fast learning curve, especially compared to skiing and surfing. You should see tremendous progress by the end of the first day.

WHAT YOU'LL NEED

- *ski resort that allows snowboarding*

- *snowboard and equipment: boots, bindings, accessories (sunglasses, helmet)*

- *warm, comfortable clothes: dress in layers so you can store an extra sweater or turtleneck in a locker*

- *lessons from a professional snowboarder*

$$$$ EXPENSIVE (OVER $75)

 GO ONLINE

Key Internet search words: Ski Resorts, Snowboarding Lessons

 GREAT DATE DETAILS

Step 1: *Locate a nearby ski resort and book snowboarding lessons.*

Step 2: *Rent, don't buy, your equipment the first few times out. When you try on boots, though, make sure they fit right. (You don't want to be hobbled by blisters the first day.)*

Step 3: *Rent or borrow wrist guards. Most broken bones happen when boarders try to break their fall by sticking out their arms, but this maneuver often results in the facture of one or both wrists.*

Step 4: *Trust our advice here: Leave the instruction to the professionals and take a snowboard class from the local ski school.*

Become Fat~ Tire Fanatics: Go Mountain Biking

While mountain biking is one of those grab-some-wheels-and-JUST-DO-IT sports, our inaugural blaze down a trail as a couple taught us a valuable lesson: (Inexperience + Pride + Pedals) x Tricky Mountain Trails = DISASTER. Let's just say that our afternoon of multiple face-plants and bone-jarring body dabs made our date, well, "memorable." But you'll have a great time if you follow two rules of the road: (1) Never tackle more trail than you can handle and (2) don't be kamikazes—defined by those in the sport as "idiots who scream down trails, endangering the physical and mental safety of others."

WHAT YOU'LL NEED

- *two mountain bikes (popular brands include Cannondale, GT, Haro, Raleigh, Specialized, Trek)*

- *essential biking accessories: helmet, gloves, water bottle, pump, map*
- *other important items to bring: cell phone, high-energy snacks, sunscreen, and warm clothes (dress in layers)*

 $$$ MODERATE ($20 TO $75) IF YOU RENT BIKES, OR $$$$ EXPENSIVE (OVER $75) IF YOU PURCHASE THEM

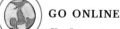 **GO ONLINE**

Key Internet search words: All-Terrain Bikes, Mountain Biking

 GREAT DATE DETAILS

Step 1: *Rent or borrow two mountain bikes, along with helmets and essential accessories.*

Step 2: *Pinpoint a safe place to ride. Above all, select a trail that fits your skill level.*

Step 3: *Tell someone exactly where you're going and when you plan to return.*

Attend an Air Show

The F-117 Nighthawk (better known as the Stealth Fighter) looks like a sleek bat as it sweeps through the clear blue sky. In the blink of an eye, it spirals to the runway, touching down in a puff of smoke. Seconds later, your ears feel as if they're going to explode as a vintage B-17 bomber rumbles overhead. And a short distance on the horizon you spot two WWII military planes staging a dog-fight. A grin stretches across your date's face, while your heart thumps with patriotism. Your afternoon date at an air show delivers nonstop adven-ture—not to mention lots to talk about.

WHAT YOU'LL NEED

- *air show event*

- *cash for entrance fee, as well as snacks and lunch*
- *appropriate clothing and accessories: jacket, hat, sunscreen, water bottle*

$$$ MODERATE ($20 TO $75)

GO ONLINE

Key Internet search words: Air Shows, Aviation Events, USA Air Shows

GREAT DATE DETAILS

Step 1: *Search your local newspaper or the Web for air shows near you. Try to find something that's no more than a two-hour drive away—unless, of course, you like road trips and would enjoy the extra time to talk. (Note that most events take place from late spring through early fall.)*

Step 2: *Beat the crowds and arrive early to the venue.*

Go Ice Fishing

Imagine the scene: The two of you all bundled up and cozy atop a frozen lake. Steam from your hot cocoa warms your cheeks as you peer into a tiny hole chipped through the ice. Maybe a hungry northern pike will chomp down on your fishing line. Maybe it'll be a big one—the fish that didn't get away. Then it happens. An otherwise tranquil moment turns chaotic as you slip and slide on the ice, reeling in the line. You put every ounce of strength into plucking dinner from the depths. And as the two of you laugh and scream, you make memories together to savor for years to come.

WHAT YOU'LL NEED

- *frozen lake (fish only in safe, designated areas)*
- *fishing rods with large guides*
- *microspinning reel*
- *line (4-8 lb. test iceline)*
- *bait: crappie minnows, wax worms, fatheads*
- *five-gallon bucket (to sit on)*

- *various fishing essentials: needle-nose pliers, bobber stops with beads, fingernail clipper (to cut line), an assortment of split shot, ice-fishing bobbers, ice scoop, jigs and spoons and hooks*
- *hand warmers*
- *fishing license and proper identification*
- *shelter and a compass*
- *blankets, gloves, hats, warm clothes*
- *snacks, hot drinks*

 ### $$$ MODERATE ($20 TO $75)

 ### GO ONLINE
Key Internet search words: Ice Fishing, Ice-Fishing Tips

 ### GREAT DATE DETAILS

Step 1: *If you're new to this sport, go with a professional. Better yet, find an ice-fishing resort near you. These places will set you up with everything you need.*

Step 2: *Borrow or rent your ice-fishing equipment.*

Step 3: *Let your family and friends know exactly where you'll be fishing and when you plan to return.*

Enjoy Full~ Throttle Fun: Spend the Day at a Race~ track

Engines roar like B-52 bombers, awaiting takeoff. Drivers sit on the grid, watching for the green light. Suddenly, the crowd is absolutely quiet. Pit crews hold their breath, photographers aim their cameras, and team managers radio last-minute details to the cockpits. The signal is given. Smoke covers the starting line, and the grandstands rumble as a pack of muscle machines tear down the track—some to victory, others to defeat. Whether it's the Grand Prix, the NASCAR circuit, or a drag-racing competition, a day at the racetrack offers thrill-a-minute fun and a chance to connect with your date.

WHAT YOU'LL NEED

- *hats, sunglasses, earplugs, sunscreen*
- *appropriate clothes*
- *plenty of cash for admission, food, and drinks*

$$$ MODERATE ($20 TO $75)

GO ONLINE

Key Internet search words: Drag Racing, Grad Prix, NASCAR

GREAT DATE DETAILS

Step 1: *In many parts of the country, auto racing is extremely popular. Consider getting your tickets ahead of time to avoid disappointments at the gate.*

Step 2: *Have fun!*

Go Windsurfing

Wind and water—that's basically all you need for this sport. Oh, and maybe a lesson or two. But once you get the hang of it, windsurfing promises outrageous fun. Salty spray peppers your face. You cruise at speeds of up to twenty miles per hour—with dolphins on your left, your date speeding by on your right, a shark on your tail. Okay, just joking about the toothy creature! (The shark, that is.)

WHAT YOU'LL NEED

- *sailboard*
- *lessons*
- *beach supplies: bathing suit, sunglasses, sunblock, water bottle*

$$$ MODERATE ($20 TO $75)

GO ONLINE

Key Internet search words: Extreme Sports, Windsurfing

GREAT DATE DETAILS

Step 1: *Pick a location. Here are three top spots to windsurf: Columbia River Gorge, Oregon; Maui, Hawaii; and the Canary Islands. You're in business if you live near any of these locations. If not, don't fret. Like we said, all you need is wind and water for this sport.*

Step 2: *Lock in your lessons. Basic windsurfing isn't difficult to learn. Two to four hours with a qualified instructor and a light breeze will get you and your date sailing on your own.*

Take on a Megacoaster

Loop, lunge, plunge, zip, flip, whirl. If your stomach can hold up, it's an awesome feeling having your mind rattled and your body flung in a zillion directions. Each summer, thrill-seeking couples flock to parks for the latest attractions. Today's megacoasters are faster, higher, and wilder—not to mention safer—and use the latest computer technology. Cars can run backward suspended below the track, and blast through dark tunnels with special effects, such as laser shows, smoke, and music.

WHAT YOU'LL NEED

- *amusement park*
- *few bucks for lunch, snacks, and drinks*
- *outdoor attire: comfortable shoes,*

clothing for the season (dress in layers), sunglasses, sunblock

$$$ MODERATE ($20 TO $75)

GO ONLINE

Key Internet search words: Amusement Parks, Megacoasters, Roller Coasters

GREAT DATE DETAILS

Step 1: *Pinpoint a place and plan your day. Is there an amusement park in your town? Will you have to drive far? What kinds of rides does your date prefer?*

Step 2: *In your quest to take on knee-knocking, bone-chilling coasters, don't forget to have plenty of downtime as well. Spend an hour at one of the park's outside cafés—sharing a sundae, people-watching, laughing, and getting to know each other.*

Surf without Seaweed: Ride a Man-made Wave

Dozens of water parks around the country feature "surfing rides." These outdoor (and indoor) attractions churn up the tide, and the adrenaline, for pro and novice surfers alike. Watch out, though: Riding the tubes at a water park can be addictive—and costly.

WHAT YOU'LL NEED

- *water park that offers surfing attractions*
- *beach attire*
- *body board (most parks provide them)*
- *plenty of cash*

$$$ MODERATE ($20 TO $75)

GO ONLINE

Key Internet search words: Flow Rider Surfing, Water Parks, Wave Machines

GREAT DATE DETAILS

Step 1: *While most water parks have wave pools, not all of them feature surfing attractions. So it's wise to call or e-mail before making plans. Here are the top North American locations that feature high-tech Flow Rider and Wave Loch rides:*

Wave House at Belmont Park (San Diego, California), Pharaoh's Lost Kingdom (Redlands, California), Kalahari Resort (Sandusky, Ohio), Kalahari Resort (Wisconsin Dells, Wisconsin), Schlitterbahn Beach Waterpark (South Padre Island, Texas), Schlitterbahn Waterpark Resort (New Braunfels, Texas), Mitchell Pool (Great Falls, Montana), Water Mania Water Theme Park (Kissimmee, Florida), Water World (Denver, Colorado), and Paramount's Kings Island (Cincinnati, Ohio).

Step 2: *Know what you and your date are getting into. How does a surfing ride work? Basically, machines shoot 100,000 gallons of water into a pool. The rushing water—only a foot deep and traveling at twenty-five miles per hour—shoots up a fiberglass outline of a wave and forms a breaking curl.*

Step 3: *Be daring and go for it—even if the two of you have never gone surfing.*

Saddle Up a Snowmobile

Whether it's backcountry exploring, flying on frozen lakes, or touring groomed trails, it's hard to beat a snowmobile for wintertime fun. Get out there and jolt some high-octane adrenaline into your relationship. Go snowmobiling.

WHAT YOU'LL NEED

- *snowmobile to rent*
- *location to ride*
- *appropriate winter attire: windproof and waterproof outer layer (jacket, pants, boots), gloves, goggles or glasses*
- *helmet*

$$$ MODERATE ($20 TO $75)

GO ONLINE

Key Internet search words:
Snowmobiling, Winter Activities

GREAT DATE DETAILS

Step 1: *Get a driving lesson before you and your date hit the trail. Above all, let someone know where you're headed.*

Step 2: *As you ride, follow the rules, especially speed limits and trail boundaries where required. It's also important that you watch out for water. (Cold temperatures can be deadly.)*

Step 3: *Always stay alert. Keep your eyes open for branches, fences, wildlife, or other obstacles.*

Hop Aboard a Helicopter

A scenic helicopter ride promises spectacular photos, especially great memories. And if you live near a natural wonder—Grand Canyon, Kauai's Na Pali Coast, Smoky Mountains—this is a must-do adventure date.

WHAT YOU'LL NEED

- *helicopter service*
- *camera*
- *sunglasses*
- *Rolaids (for bumpy rides!)*
- *extra cash for lunch or drinks*

$$$ MODERATE ($20 TO $75) TO $$$$ EXPENSIVE (OVER $75)

GO ONLINE

Key Internet search words: Helicopter Rides

GREAT DATE DETAILS

Step 1: *Reserve your ride. If you can splurge, ask about a "romance package," which may include gourmet lunch, drinks, flowers, or a photo.*

Step 2: *After your adventure, linger over drinks or a meal. Plan your next fun-filled date.*

Try Bungee Jumping

If the thought of skydiving makes your knees knock, but you long to taste the thrill of free flight, consider bungee jumping. It doesn't require hours of preparation, it's quite safe, and it's a once-in-a-lifetime experience you and your date won't stop talking about.

WHAT YOU'LL NEED

- *bungee-jumping attraction*
- *camera*
- *courage*

$$$ MODERATE ($20 TO $75)

GO ONLINE

Key Internet search words: Bungee-Jumping Attractions

GREAT DATE DETAILS

Step 1: *After pinpointing a bungee-jumping attraction near you and psyching up a bit, write down a connection between this experience and faith (and be prepared to discuss it afterward).*

Step 2: *Get this experience on film. Better yet, bring along a video camera and tape your adventure date.*

Step 3: *Spend time talking about your plunge. How is bungee jumping a lot like faith? How did you feel as you were free-falling? How do you react when life seems out of control?*

*Yours, O Lᴏʀᴅ, is the greatness
and the power and the glory
and the majesty and the splendor,
for everything in heaven and earth is yours.
Yours, O Lᴏʀᴅ, is the kingdom;
you are exalted as head over all.
Wealth and honor come from you;
you are the ruler of all things.
In your hands are strength and power
to exalt and give strength to all.*

1 Cʜʀᴏɴɪᴄʟᴇs 29:11-12

CHAPTER 3
Highly Cultured Dates

It's exciting to put on your
finest clothes and escape to a
five-star event: the ballet, an art
show, the fanciest restaurant in town,
a fund-raiser for a worthy cause.
This chapter is packed with classy
ideas for highly cultured dates.

Treat Yourselves to the Symphony

W. A. Mozart wrote, "To reach the heavens is wonderful and sublime; but on dear earth life is also amazing and astonishing! So let us remain mere mortals." Close your eyes and imagine a concert hall filled with the heavenly sounds of Mozart—or other great music masters: Bach, Beethoven, Handel, Pachelbel, Tchaikovsky, Vivaldi. An evening at the symphony tops our list for a date filled with fine art, culture, and class.

WHAT YOU'LL NEED

- *tickets to the symphony*
- *formal attire*
- *extra cash for dinner and drinks*

$$$$ EXPENSIVE (OVER $75)

 GO ONLINE

Key Internet search words: Classical Music, Symphony

 GREAT DATE DETAILS

Step 1: *Go online and find out what symphony is playing in a concert hall near you.*

Step 2: *Learn what appeals to your date and buy your tickets.*

Step 3: *Wear your finest clothes—a tuxedo or formal dress.*

Step 4: *Enjoy a fine meal before heading to the symphony.*

Experience an Art Gallery

The Museum of Modern Art in New York City is a place where you can gaze at van Gogh's Starry Night. Several hundred miles away at the Denver Art Museum, you can study some of world's best exhibits of Native American art. The fact is, countless museums from coast to coast will enrich your life and transport your imaginations into the amazing depths of human creativity. Make a date at an art gallery.

WHAT YOU'LL NEED

- *tickets to an art gallery (at some locations, Saturday entrance is often free to locals)*

- *extra cash for lunch and drinks*

- *willingness to step out of your comfort zone and learn something new*

$$ INEXPENSIVE ($10 TO $20)

 GO ONLINE

Key Internet search words: Art Exhibits, Art Galleries, Museums of Art

 GREAT DATE DETAILS

Step 1: *Go online and find out what's being displayed at art galleries in your area.*

Step 2: *Buy your tickets or take advantage of "free Saturdays." In some parts of the country, just flash your driver's licenses, and the entrance fee is on the house.*

Step 3: *Be prepared to experience some amazing art and cultural exhibits. As you linger in the museum, ask your date some questions: "What's your favorite style of art and why?" "Have you ever tried to paint or sculpt something?"*

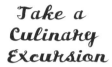

Take a Culinary Excursion

Nothing beats a five-course meal at a five-star establishment. Regardless of where you dine, choose a restaurant that tops the scale when it comes to charm, views, environment, service, and fine food.

WHAT YOU'LL NEED

- *a restaurant with character*
- *formal attire*
- *willingness to spend a chunk of change*

$$$$ EXPENSIVE (OVER $75)

GO ONLINE

Key Internet search words: Award-Winning Restaurants, Culinary Picks, Fine Dining

GREAT DATE DETAILS

Step 1: *List several fine-dining possibilities in your area. Check the Web for reviews. Compare notes with friends.*

Step 2: *Take a risk and try something different, maybe ethnic cuisine.*

Step 3: *Make a reservation, then prepare your date for a memorable dining experience.*

Take a Stroll Down Broadway: Treat Your~selves to Live Theater

Drama, comedy, musical, ballet, opera: Live theater offers a wealth of possibilities for a priceless experience.

WHAT YOU'LL NEED

- *tickets to a theater production*
- *attire fitting the dress code*
- *cash for meals and drinks*

$$$$ EXPENSIVE (OVER $75)

GO ONLINE

Key Internet search words: Ballet, Broadway Productions, Musicals, Theater, Opera

GREAT DATE DETAILS

Step 1: *Learn what kind of theater appeals to your date: highbrow opera, glitzy Broadway-style musicals, avant-garde student productions.*

Step 2: *If the event is formal, go with elegant evening wear. If the venue has an artsy, casual feel, go funky. (Coordinate with your date.)*

Step 3: *Top off your time together with coffee and dessert.*

Experience a Romantic Hot Air Balloon Ride

Picture you and your date gazing at an enormous, multicolored balloon as you climb into its basket. The pilot presses a propane burner, which roars like an angry dragon. The balloon rises, then drifts through the air. The scenery below is breathtaking: a coastline, desert, or misty hills. Regardless of where you ride, an excursion in a hot-air balloon is a highly classy date.

WHAT YOU'LL NEED

- *company offering hot-air balloon rides*
- *warm clothes*
- *camera*

$$$$ EXPENSIVE (OVER $75)

 GO ONLINE

Key Internet search words: Balloon Festivals, Hot-Air Balloon Rides

 GREAT DATE DETAILS

Step 1: *As you schedule your trip, inquire about special romance packages including meal, drinks, flowers, and a portrait.*

Step 2: *Get set for an unforgettable day.*

Flee from sexual immorality.
All other sins a man commits are
outside his body, but he who sins
sexually sins against his own body.
Do you not know that your body is a temple
of the Holy Spirit, who is in you,
whom you have received from God?
You are not your own;
you were bought at a price.
Therefore honor God with your body.

1 Corinthians 6:18-20

CHAPTER 4
Dates While You Wait

Ever feel like you're the only one who's trying to follow God's plan for purity? Sometimes it can feel terribly lonely staying obedient to our Lord. Come to think of it, in most areas of morality, it's often harder to do what's right than to do what's wrong. But get this: You're not alone. There's a moral revolution of young people who are willing to wait. This chapter celebrates your commitment to purity with creative dates that are grounded in wholesome fun!

Make a Bookstore Date

Spend time at a bookstore, and choose devotional guides for each other. Then linger over tea or coffee, sharing an entry.

WHAT YOU'LL NEED

- *local bookstore that sells Christian products*
- *cash*

$$$ MODERATE ($20 TO $75)

GO ONLINE

Key Internet search words: Bookstore Outlets, Christian Booksellers

GREAT DATE DETAILS

Step 1: *Share goals for your time together. Discuss reasons for picking a particular book, and even express hopes and prayers for each other and your relationship.*

Step 2: *Allow time to pick out books for each other (minimum forty-five minutes).*

Step 3: *Find a quiet corner—maybe with comfy overstuffed chairs. Order hot drinks and share devotions, thoughts, and prayers.*

Babysit Together

Give a married couple the afternoon off, and spend time with the *Blues Clues* crowd. Make babysitting a Saturday adventure.

WHAT YOU'LL NEED

- *family to rescue*
- *a plan for the afternoon*
- *patience*

$ CHEAP (UNDER $10)

GO ONLINE

Key Internet search words: Babysitting Tips, Children's Interests, Toddlers

GREAT DATE DETAILS

Step 1: *Lock in details with the parents, and make certain your date is up for the challenge.*

Step 2: *Consider activities to do with the child. Can the child play outside? What kinds of DVDs are acceptable? What food must you prepare?*

Step 3: *Your primary concern is the child's well-being. Pay attention to how your date interacts with the child, including patience and attitude.*

Step 4: *End the day by talking about your experience.*

Pet Sit

Maybe someone you know needs a pet care-taker for the weekend. Feeding, bathing, or walking a pet can offer a fun-filled way for you to spend time together. Learning how your partner handles an animal offers insight into his or her personality.

WHAT YOU'LL NEED

- *pet to befriend*
- *lots of love*

$ CHEAP (UNDER $10)

GO ONLINE

Key Internet search words: Pet Owner's Tips, Pet Sitting

GREAT DATE DETAILS

Step 1: *Interact with the pet, and involve your date in the process. Ask your partner to help you take the dog for a walk or entertain a feline with cat toys.*

Step 2: *Use this experience to connect with your date. Ask about childhood pets and favorite animals.*

Hide a Dozen Love Notes

Place a dozen love notes throughout your date's bedroom. The last one should be the biggest and brightest. This message will instruct your date to meet for a very special date.

WHAT YOU'LL NEED

- *twelve cards*
- *dinner reservations*
- *friends who can help distract your date*
- *cell phone*

$$$ MODERATE ($20 TO $75)

GO ONLINE

Key Internet search words: Cards, Creative Love Notes, Romantic Restaurants (in Your Town)

GREAT DATE DETAILS

Step 1: *After you've filled out your notes, make dinner reservations at your favorite restaurant or reserve concert tickets.*

Step 2: *Celebrate your commitment to God and to purity. Write words of encouragement, telling your date how special he or she is to the Lord and to you. Communicate how much you respect and cherish this special person.*

Step 3: *Have a friend create a diversion to get your date out of the house for an hour. This friend should ensure that your date sees the cards and details of your dinner or theater plans.*

Step 4: *Wait for your date to call.*

Get Dirty for God: Volunteer During a Church Workday

Consider volunteering at a church workday: painting the sanctuary, scrubbing floors, cleaning nursery toys. But as you roll up your sleeves and break a sweat together, you'll discover each other's heart for God.

WHAT YOU'LL NEED

- *service location*
- *work clothes*
- *desire to serve*
- *cash for food afterward*

$ CHEAP (UNDER $10)

GO ONLINE

Key Internet search words: Christian Service

GREAT DATE DETAILS

Step 1: *Pinpoint a place to serve side by side.*

Step 2: *Study Matthew 25:31-46 and pray together beforehand.*

Step 3: *During the workday, ask questions: "What's the most unusual service project you've done?" "Have you ever been on a missions trip?"*

Step 4: *Relax over dinner. Talk about the day.*

Go on a "Mission Impossible" Date

Your assignment, should you choose to accept it, is to pull out the stops on creativity and to treat your date to a day of mystery, adventure, and imagination.

WHAT YOU'LL NEED

- *cassette and cassette recorder*
- *car and driver*
- *dress clothes and casual wear*
- *cash*

$$$$ EXPENSIVE (OVER $75)

GO ONLINE

Key Internet search words: Local Entertainment, Recreation, Restaurants

GREAT DATE DETAILS

Step 1: *Pick an eight-hour block of time and ask your partner to bring extra clothes—from casual to dressy.*

Step 2: *Plan every detail from start to finish. For example: (1) breakfast at Starbucks, (2) laser tag, (3) lunch at a five-star restaurant, then (4) a movie.*

Step 3: *Recruit a friend to be your chauffer.*

Step 4: *Record your "Mission Impossible" message: "Your assignment, should you choose to accept it, is to join me for a day of adventure. . . ."*

Step 5: *On the day of your date, your chauffer drops you off at a coffeehouse then picks up your partner, handing him or her an envelope with the recorded message before escorting him or her to the breakfast spot.*

Host a Super Bowl Party

All you need are sodas, snacks, a TV, and friends. Plan this party with your partner—make it a date! The two of you will share some laughs as you root for your favorite team.

WHAT YOU'LL NEED

- *TV and location big enough for several people*
- *snacks and drinks*
- *decorations*

$$$ MODERATE ($20 TO $75)

GO ONLINE

Key Internet search words: Party Foods, Super Bowl Party Ideas

GREAT DATE DETAILS

Step 1: *Pick a location for your party and send invitations. Plan and talk through every detail.*

Step 2: *Buy sodas and snacks to feed your hungry crowd.*

Step 3: *On the day of your party, deck out your location with Super Bowl-themed decorations.*

Step 4: *Have fun!*

Share Random Acts of Love: Serve the Needy Together

Regardless of the need, you and your partner can touch someone's life: a lonely shut-in who yearns for companionship or an overextended single parent who desperately needs a break from the kids.

WHAT YOU'LL NEED

- *person to serve*
- *cash for lunch*

$ CHEAP (UNDER $10)

GO ONLINE

Key Internet search words: Christian Service

GREAT DATE DETAILS

Step 1: *Brainstorm together for places to serve and people to bless.*

Step 2: *Choose someone to help. Should you prepare lunch? Will your time involve cleaning, mowing, or yard work? Will you give a parent a break?*

Step 3: *Afterward, have lunch together. Make it a devotional time and study Romans 12:10–11, 13.*

Write a Customized Devo (Then Share It)

Think about your partner: Who is this person? Characteristics, qualities, spiritual gifts? Which Scripture or Bible character comes to mind? How do you pray for him or her? Put these thoughts on paper, then share them during a special "devo date."

WHAT YOU'LL NEED

- *Bible*
- *blank card to write out your devo*
- *cash for lunch or snacks*

$ CHEAP (UNDER $10)

GO ONLINE

Key Internet search words: Christian Books, Devotionals, Devotions

GREAT DATE DETAILS

Step 1: *Buy a blank card to write your devotion.*

Step 2: *Put together your custom devo using your Bible and favorite devotionals.*

Step 3: *Call your partner and make a date.*

Step 4: *Meet for lunch and share what you've written.*

Create Next~to~New Care Packages

Most of us accumulate more stuff than we need. Here's an idea that lets you and your date bless the life of another with something you no longer need.

WHAT YOU'LL NEED

- *items to give away: clothes, toys, books, collectibles*
- *gift bags, ribbons*

$ CHEAP (UNDER $10)

GO ONLINE

Key Internet search words: Christian Charities, Donations

GREAT DATE DETAILS

Step 1: *Call your date and brainstorm items to give away, as well as charities or people to give them to.*

Step 2: *Collect, clean, and bag your items, perhaps in stylish gift bags.*

Step 3: *Deliver your care packages.*

Step 4: Afterward, grab sodas and talk about the experience.

*Let us hold unswervingly to the hope
we profess, for he who promised is faithful.
And let us consider how we may spur one
another on toward love and good deeds.
Let us not give up meeting together,
as some are in the habit of doing,
but let us encourage one another—and all
the more as you see the Day approaching.*

HEBREWS 10:23-25

CHAPTER 5
Group Dates

While traditional dating is one-on-one and accompanied by such things as a romantic atmosphere, sweaty palms, and the desire to sound intelligent, a group date is quite different. It takes place with friends. It's also less formal, has almost no romantic atmosphere, and is nearly pressure free. In other words, you've got a better chance to be yourself. This chapter is packed with tons of great group date ideas.

Host a Cookout

Pull out the badminton net, volleyball, and horseshoes. Ask every couple to bring a dish, then fire up the grill!

WHAT YOU'LL NEED

- *grill(s)*
- *space for several couples*
- *ice cooler*
- *plates, cups, napkins, utensils*
- *yard games*

\$\$ INEXPENSIVE (\$10 TO \$15) PER COUPLE

GO ONLINE

Key Internet search words: Grilling Techniques, Backyard Parties, Group Games

GREAT DATE DETAILS

Step 1: *Make an invitation list together. Divide food and supplies among those invited.*

Step 2: *Clean the grill(s) and mow the lawn.*

Step 3: *Assign each couple a task: flipping burgers, refilling the ice, or refereeing games.*

Step 4: *Arrange seating so folks can chat.*

Step 5: *Thank God for a summer barbecue.*

Create a Fruit Basket

Fruit—nature's candy. Giving a fresh-fruit gift to an elderly person is healthy, fun, from the heart.

WHAT YOU'LL NEED

- *beautiful basket*
- *variety of fruit*
- *colorful plastic wrap*
- *bow*

$$$ MODERATE ($20 TO $75)

GO ONLINE

Key Internet search words: Fruit Arrangements, Gift Giving, How to Make a Bow

GREAT DATE DETAILS

Step 1: *Shop together for supplies and fruit.*

Step 2: *Place the fruit in the basket leaving the bananas on top.*

Step 3: *Wrap the basket in plastic wrap, gathering the corners above the basket.*

Step 4: *Have each couple deliver a basket to its recipient with a warm smile and friendly hug. Stay to chat if invited.*

Go to an Amusement Park

Are you crazy about a Ferris wheel, bumper cars, or cotton candy? Head to an amusement park with your date and other friends.

WHAT YOU'LL NEED

- *money for entrance, tickets, and food*
- *comfortable clothes and shoes*
- *park map*

$$$ MODERATE ($20 TO $75)

GO ONLINE

Key Internet search words: Amusement Parks, Tourist Attractions, Maps and Directions, Local Weather

GREAT DATE DETAILS

Step 1: *Set a date and time to carpool to the park.*

Step 2: *That morning check the weather and directions.*

Step 3: *Arrive as park doors open.*

Step 4: *Reserve time alone for you and your date to enjoy a ride or meal.*

Step 5: *Experience as many different rides and shows that time allows.*

Clean Up a Neighbor's Yard

Is there someone who needs help in your neighborhood? Organize a few couples and get your neighbor's permission to help with yard work.

WHAT YOU'LL NEED

- *homeowner's permission*
- *several helpers*
- *rakes, bags, wheelbarrow, clippers*
- *friendly smile*

$ CHEAP (UNDER $10)

GO ONLINE

Key Internet search words: Lawn Maintenance, Volunteer Opportunities

GREAT DATE DETAILS

Step 1: *Together, ask the home-owner's permission. Then schedule the big cleanup with friends.*

Step 2: *Show up with supplies. Ask your friends to bring items they may have.*

Step 3: *This is a labor of love. Rake, cut, and trim with pride.*

Step 4: *Thank the homeowner for the opportunity to help.*

Step 5: *Hit your local burger joint to appease a well-deserved appetite.*

Go to a Water Park

Nothing takes the bite out of summer heat like big slides and splashing in the waves. Spend a day at a water park.

WHAT YOU'LL NEED

- *water park*
- *modest bathing suits*
- *good friends*

$$$ MODERATE ($20 TO $75)

GO ONLINE

Key Internet search words: Parks and Recreation, Local Weather, Water Parks, Maps and Directions

GREAT DATE DETAILS

Step 1: *Find out the cost, operating hours, and directions to a water park.*

Step 2: *With your date, call and invite friends. Set a time and make sure everyone can ride comfortably.*

Step 3: *Splash, dive, and take on the biggest waterslide.*

Step 4: *Meet at the snack bar for lunch.*

Step 5: *Save enough energy for the drive home!*

Beat the Boredom Blahs with Board Games

Dig out those board games and have a party. It may seem old-fashioned, but there's a reason they've been around for so long. They're fun! Most games are designed for two to eight players requiring a little skill and a whole lot of luck.

WHAT YOU'LL NEED

- *one or more board games*
- *cozy room*
- *food and drinks*

$ CHEAP (UNDER $10)

GO ONLINE

Key Internet search words: Board Games, Game Rules, Party Appetizers

GREAT DATE DETAILS

Step 1: *Make a date and invite your friends to enjoy your families' old board games.*

Step 2: *Prepare snacks and drinks beforehand so you can join the fun.*

Step 3: *Have more than one game going if enough people play.*

'Tis the Season to Give

Every day is a good day to give gifts. But Christmas seems to be the time dedicated to sharing the wealth. Most churches have organized activities that include creating and delivering gifts and food baskets to others in the community. Volunteer to be God's hands and feet by delivering goodies.

WHAT YOU'LL NEED

- *group that needs help delivering Christmas baskets*
- *transportation*
- *good map*
- *cell phone (optional)*

$$ INEXPENSIVE ($20 TO $75)

GO ONLINE

Key Internet search words: Church Activities, Maps and Directions, Volunteer Opportunities

GREAT DATE DETAILS

Step 1: *Find out if your church has plans to deliver Christmas gifts. If not, volunteer with another group.*

Step 2: *Contact enough friends to help out.*

Step 3: *Get directions and a phone number before leaving on a delivery.*

Step 4: *Go in groups of four, and take turns knocking on the door.*

Step 5: *Smile and be friendly. You represent the hard work of preparing this holiday gift.*

Step 6: *Get together afterward with the other volunteers for a celebratory lunch.*

Celebrate as Christmas Carolers

Oh, the joys of Christmas! The holidays are filled with shopping, wrapping, and other activities. One old-time favorite is Christmas caroling. Call your friends, find some song lyrics, and spread the joy. You'll love it!

WHAT YOU'LL NEED

- *Christmas song books or printed sheet music*
- *warm clothing: hat, coat, gloves, warm footwear*
- *flashlight*
- *joyful heart*
- *cookies and hot chocolate*

$ CHEAP (UNDER $10)

 GO ONLINE

Key Internet search words: Christmas Carols, Hymn Lyrics, Favorite Christmas Songs

 GREAT DATE DETAILS

Step 1: *Call friends and family who would like to participate. Encourage everyone to bring a flashlight.*

Step 2: *Decide which homes or neighborhoods to visit. Meet as a group and carpool. Have snacks ready for your return.*

Step 3: *Pass out songbooks.*

Step 4: *Gather outside a home, have one person ring the doorbell, and sing two or three beautiful songs. Finish with "We Wish You a Merry Christmas." Wish them God's blessings and move on to the next house.*

Step 5: *At the end of the evening, enjoy a time of fellowship and laughter with warm cookies and hot cocoa.*

Go Crazy for March Madness

Heat intensifies as thirty-two narrows to sixteen, then eight, then the final four, which delivers the top two, and finally the champion. March Madness is one of the most exciting college ball events, when young basketball players vie for the national title, supported by millions of fans. Grab some friends and join the hype.

WHAT YOU'LL NEED

- *roster of games*
- *cable or satellite TV*
- *comfy room*
- *snacks*

$$ INEXPENSIVE ($10 TO $20)

GO ONLINE

Key Internet search words: College Basketball, March Madness, ESPN

GREAT DATE DETAILS

Step 1: *Locate a March Madness schedule. Check to see if you have the right TV channels. If not, most cable companies offer a special temporary package.*

Step 2: *Pick a time when several games will be played back to back.*

Step 3: *Invite your date and other friends over.*

Step 4: *Ask your date if he or she would be interested in helping set up for the party—a little quality time together before the craziness begins.*

Step 5: *Adjust the furniture so everyone can comfortably see the action.*

Step 6: *Pull out the food and turn on the games. Don't worry, even nonfans will get caught up in the madness.*

Tube It

Think of nature as a really large playground. Inner-tubing down a creek, stream, or river is a great way to find relief on a hot day. Tubes are easy to come by, and most small waterways are free. A slow, scenic route can offer a safe and enjoyable ride.

WHAT YOU'LL NEED

- *one inner tube per person*
- *air pump (or access to one)*
- *creek, stream, or river*
- *sunblock*

$ CHEAP (UNDER $10)

GO ONLINE

Key Internet search words: Local Waterways, Maps, Outdoor Sports, Water Safety

GREAT DATE DETAILS

Step 1: *Locate a local waterway. Call your law enforcement agency and inquire about restrictions, guidelines, or hidden dangers of the route.*

Step 2: *Call friends and find old inner tubes. Gas stations are a good source of tubes and air pumps.*

Step 3: *Before entering the water, be sure everyone knows the route and safety tips. It's a good idea to wear shoes and sunscreen.*

Step 4: *Plan ahead. Provide enough automobiles at the end to transport everyone and their tubes to the beginning. Otherwise, a relaxing float will end in a long walk home.*

Step 5: *Jump in and enjoy the view from the water.*

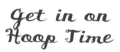

Get in on Hoop Time

It's the top of the top, the cream of the crop, the NBA! This fast-paced game delivers thrills up to the last seconds. Better yet, it can be enjoyed in any weather. So grab a hot dog and soda, and hold on for sixty minutes of nonstop competition.

WHAT YOU'LL NEED

- *game tickets*
- *transportation*
- *binoculars (if seated in the nosebleed section)*
- *clothes matching team colors*

$$$$ EXPENSIVE (OVER $75)

GO ONLINE

Key Internet search words: NBA, Tickets, Game Schedule, Maps and Directions, Arena Parking

GREAT DATE DETAILS

Step 1: *Get the schedule of the closest NBA team to your hometown.*

Step 2: *Call the arena, look in the newspaper, or go online to check availability and cost of tickets. Spread the information to friends.*

Step 3: *Once everyone has tickets, arrange transportation. These are fun activities to prepare with your date.*

Step 4: *Game Day—Find clothes in your home team's colors.*

Step 5: *Leave early enough to allow for traffic.*

Step 6: *Once you find your seats, load up on food and enjoy the game.*

Send Treats to Soldiers

There's nothing like the taste of homemade cookies, the feel of a full toothpaste tube, or the value of a book of stamps. Okay, maybe not on a regular day, but if you are in the service overseas, small comforts from home are hard to come by. A care package can boost morale for weeks.

WHAT YOU'LL NEED

- *strong box with lid, packing material, and tape*
- *military address(es)*
- *imperishable items (and candy and cookies)*
- *letter or card*

$$ INEXPENSIVE ($10 TO $20) PER COUPLE

GO ONLINE

Key Internet search words: USO, Local Newspaper, Overseas Shipping Requirements

GREAT DATE DETAILS

Step 1: *Soldiers, sailors, and marines are beyond our borders in both peace- and wartime. Contact the USO, the newspaper, your church, or family of a soldier for contact information.*

Step 2: *Take on no more than ten boxes your first time.*

Step 3: *Spread the wealth. After deciding what to send, gather items among the group. Toothpaste, stamps, disposable razors, cookies, gum, cards, and hometown newspapers are hits.*

Step 4: *Pack each box carefully for the long trip. A deployed soldier's address is always stateside; the military delivers the rest of the way.*

Step 5: *Include a card signed by your group.*

Throw a Surprise Party

Does someone you know have a birthday coming up? If so, then it's time for a big ol' surprise party. Planning in secrecy may be harder, but it's well worth it.

WHAT YOU'LL NEED

- *invitation list*
- *party location*
- *food and cake*
- *decorations*
- *cups, plates, forks, napkins*

$$$ MODERATE ($20 TO $75)

GO ONLINE

Key Internet search words: Party Supplies, Theme Parties, Park Reservations, Conference Room Reservations, Birthday Cakes

GREAT DATE DETAILS

Step 1: *Invite as many people as your budget allows. On average, only about half will show up.*

Step 1: *Order the cake at least a week in advance.*

Step 3: *One person should be in charge of each area (cake, decorating, snacks, invitations, cleanup).*

Step 4: *Luring the birthday boy or girl to the spot at the precise time should be arranged in advance.*

Step 5: *When the person arrives, join in on a loud SURPRISE! Snap a picture of his or her shocked expression.*

Host a Watch Night Service

Three, two, one—Happy New Year! There are many ways to roll in the New Year. Make this year special by hosting a midnight watch party. Play games, eat junk food, and bring in the New Year with prayer. Set aside at least thirty minutes at midnight to talk with God. Thank Him for the past year and pray for His guidance during the coming one. There's no better way to usher in a new year.

WHAT YOU'LL NEED

- *party location*
- *invitations*
- *food, caffeinated drinks*
- *cups, plates, forks*

$$$ MODERATE (\$20 TO \$75)

GO ONLINE

Key Internet search words: New Year's Eve, Party Decorations, Prayers and Poems, Party Supplies

GREAT DATE DETAILS

Step 1: *Find a location for both a party and prayer.*

Step 2: *With your date, send out invitations via e-mail, telephone, snail mail, or a personal visit.*

Step 3: *Gather food, supplies, and music. Remind everyone that you plan to usher in the New Year with prayer.*

Step 4: *No later than 11:45 p.m., turn off the music, close the doors, and have everyone find comfortable spots. Lead with prayer, Scripture reading, and testimonies. Allow God to come in and lead the way. Allow at least thirty minutes for prayer.*

Step 5: *Upon completion, turn the music back on and continue celebrating. Make sure everyone has a safe way home. There are a lot of crazy drivers out there around 1:00 a.m.*

Do not let your hearts be troubled.
Trust in God; trust also in me.
In my Father's house are many rooms;
if it were not so, I would have told you.
I am going there to prepare a place for you.
And if I go and prepare a place for you,
I will come back and take you to be with me
that you also may be where I am.
You know the way to the place
where I am going.

JOHN 14:1-4

CHAPTER 6
Long~Distance Dates

Dating long-distance can be difficult, but not impossible. So how can you stay connected when there are hundreds of miles between you? This chapter is filled with ideas that are anything but ordinary.

IM and a DVD

It's not as personal as sitting next to your date in a movie theater, but this idea is the next best thing. It's also a great way to melt away those miles that separate you.

WHAT YOU'LL NEED

- *movie on DVD (or video) identical to one your date possesses*
- *ability to send instant messages by phone or computer*
- *popcorn, sodas, snacks*

$ CHEAP (UNDER $10)

GO ONLINE

Key Internet search words: DVD Rentals, Movie Reviews

GREAT DATE DETAILS

Step 1: *Agree upon a movie, then set aside a block of uninterrupted time.*

Step 2: *Pick up your flick at a DVD/video store.*

Step 3: *On date day, serve up popcorn or chips and soda, and cue up your movie.*

Step 4: *Contact your date and synchronize your watches. You must begin your movie at exactly the same time.*

Step 5: *Kick back and enjoy the show "together." Agree to IM each other at certain points during the movie—sharing what you like and don't like about the flick, and what you think will happen next.*

Step 6: *After the movie, call your partner and follow up on your date.*

Piece Together a "Puzzle Portrait"

Maybe puzzles are something your little brother gets excited about. But consider the romantic possibilities: You both send custom "puzzle photos" of yourselves, then spend a few hours by phone as you put them together. When the last piece is in place, your date has a portrait for the wall.

WHAT YOU'LL NEED

- *separate portraits of each of you*
- *photo shop that can make puzzle pieces*
- *postage*

$$$ MODERATE ($20 TO $75)

GO ONLINE

Key Internet search words: Puzzle Portraits

GREAT DATE DETAILS

Step 1: *Go online or call a photo-processing store or local printer and inquire about custom photo products. Many can create mugs, T-shirts, and puzzles. Have two puzzles created from your portraits. Let the image be a surprise.*

Step 2: *Keep one puzzle, and send the other to your partner. Make plans for your long-distance date.*

Step 3: *On the day of your date, communicate by phone. As you work separately, talk about what's been going on in your life, school, work—the challenges of piecing together this "crazy puzzle." Do your best to not divulge the image—at least at the beginning!*

Step 4: *As the picture comes into focus and the last piece is put in place, instruct your partner on how to turn the puzzle into a poster. Refer to the instructions given by the photo shop that created it.*

Concluding Thoughts about Love and Dating

Males and females are attractive to each other. . . . However, males and females are also very different. Bringing two unique people together in genuine love requires that they try to understand each other— understand the differences as well as the common ground. That takes communication.

JOHN C. MAXWELL

Love is patient, love is kind. It does not envy, it does not boast, it is not proud. It is not rude, it is not self-seeking, it is not easily angered, it keeps no record of wrongs. Love does not delight in evil but rejoices with the truth. It always protects, always trusts, always hopes, always perseveres.

1 CORINTHIANS 13:4–7

ACKNOWLEDGMENTS

Michael and Tiffany Ross would like to thank two special family members who assisted with this book:

Bonnie Cox—A mother of three daughters, the wife of the late Floyd Cox, an admired community leader in Pineville, West Virginia, and an amazingly creative writer. Bonnie absolutely adores her grandson, Christopher. She also has a fond spot in her heart for the many elementary school children she cares for.

Theresa Cox—Writer and professor at Eastern Virginia Medical School in Norfolk, Virginia. Tess has recently completed her MA in counseling at Regent University. She lives in a beach house on the shores of the Chesapeake Bay. Her favorite authors are J. R. R. Tolkien, C. S. Lewis, Henri Nouwen, and Rich Mullins.